The Scheme of Things

The Scheme of Things

Hilde Weisert

David Robert Books

© 2015 by Hilde Weisert

Published by David Robert Books
P.O. Box 541106
Cincinnati, OH 45254-1106

Typeset in Garamond by WordTech Communications LLC, Cincinnati, OH

ISBN: 9781625491510
LCCN: 2015948135

Poetry Editor: Kevin Walzer
Business Editor: Lori Jareo

Visit us on the web at www.davidrobertbooks.com

Acknowledgements

CALYX magazine (winner, Lois Cranston Memorial Prize, 2008) and the Wilfred Owen Journal, "Finding Wilfred Owen Again"

Cincinnati Review, "Mercy"

Independent Weekly, "In Sasebo, Nagasaki" (published as "Everything Betrays Me Now")

Ironwood, "Coney Island Elegy"

Litchfield Review, "A Wonderful Life"

Lips, "Resist Regret," "The Secret Hand," "The Truth of Art"

Paterson Literary Review, "Berkshire Summer"; Honorable Mention, 2013 Allen Ginsberg Poetry Awards

Plume Poetry, "The Transit Hall on Pier 86"

Prairie Schooner, "Where We Were and What We Were Doing"

Qu Literary Journal, "The Best Funeral Ever," "The Year of Reading Yeats"

The Cortland Review, "Grandfather, Balloon"

The Sun, "Imagination Itself," "One Good New Poem"

Writ, "The Scheme of Things"

The author wishes to acknowledge with gratitude the Virginia Center for the Creative Arts and the New Jersey State Council on the Arts for fellowships which supported the writing of poems in this collection.

Contents

Where We Were and What We Were Doing

The Scheme of Things

An old idea in light of recent evidence

Lacunae lace the fossil record, and coeval bones
of super- and subordinate species—the one
we'd thought replaced the other—won't line up
for the slow, steady march, where the primal
versions (short of reach, or range, or wit required
for the shifting fruit, or prey, or plight) would retire
with the resigned sigh of the marginally outclassed.
Instead, ingenious leapers coexist with their irrupted past.

So: One morning, from nowhere, an unselected self: A gait
that unrhythms you, a grasp that fills your fist
with nameless stuff. Your skull a holy dome—A new weight!
But on this plain, the claw-and-hunch will coexist
with you for ages. All aching appetite, her jaws will snap
flesh, and your fine teeth close. Even now, ontogeny recaps.

THREE STARS

The Certainty of Others

"…The certainty of others, the life, love, sight, hearing of others.
Others will enter the gates of the ferry and cross from shore to shore…"

-- Walt Whitman, "Crossing Brooklyn Ferry"

Soon we are to leave this year, and century, a crossing
my grandmother made as a young woman—but she was brave,
hands eager on the rail, eyes brimming as a new continent
wheeled its great machine into view, the New York World
copper and a rising dome, the new shapes a skyline.

Was there no one she loved in that old wooden land,
no one to make her feel that what she left
was not behind an ocean, but below?
I fear for those who stayed, how they can go on so far
from where we rise now on the new world's turning…

And yet lower Manhattan is always lovely from the Heights:
The white choirs my father down from Dartmouth saw in '29.
As late as '68, dragging home winter grocery sacks, my roommate
caught a glimpse of the Singer and thought it was a Christmas tree on
    fire.
I don't remember when they took the Singer down.

It is only Brooklyn, and the lesser river, yet standing here
I feel that it is time we look across, and that this briny island
has sailed us in, the salt wind of a century on our faces.
But it is Brooklyn. I see the ferries run again, the white wakes
returning home. And behind, only a century leaving us.

The Transit Hall on Pier 86

They say there's a place in the brain for faces
and I believe it, this headache a claw
into raw nerves, the strain of testing
so many men's faces for my one "Father"

as the boat empties and the transit hall
fills with women, children, and one plausible man
after another whose face dissolves
with study. For a moment each one

could be him, ruddy, regular, a gaze returned
into my face, which has its own brain
place also working hard to make
something recognizable as a daughter

out of so many raw nerves. The looking and the looked-at
swim—these places in the brain are wet, gelid,
something out of Coelenterata that starts to wave
at this handsome new father until his hard

square eyes break my floundering smile
into one more mistake. A decade is long
when you are twenty. The long hall rings
with "Hello's!", feet on pavement, the clamoring

embrace. When I see him, I am alone,
and at his eyes, drop my own, ashamed
I tried so many strangers on, itinerants against

the one face that goes here, and whose eyes

I could have lost when they are the same
as mine. Mine that I work to raise, bringing up
a woman's face out of a child's, and offering my father
a hand, dry and outstretched.

Three Stars

In Paris together after twenty years, we walk half the map by one,
Porte Maillot down a zig-and-zag diagonal to our old Café Verdun.
We walk, and the Plan's red-and-black lines block-by-block unflatten
into real-life streets, the smell of bread, and children wearing hats;
ancient echoing courtyards and the earthy exhalations of the Metro
    stations.
We walk alike, with ease, but talk like strangers stumbling through
  translation.
Still, I'm restored, quenched by northern light like water,
alive and on foot in Paris, remembering, zig by zag, what it was to be
    your daughter

long ago. When you brought us here, your little woolen family in the
    gloom,
the grit of war on walls, Europe was as strange as Asia, and yet made
    for us.
You weren't much of a father, Father, but I eat Verdun's carrot-
    leek potage
and the gritty long-lost warmth salves everything. How we made
    this home,
and then could leave, and how you shook your fist (You'd paid for us!)
is beyond me, mon père. Quand-même! I give your page three stars:
    Vaut le voyage.

Buda-Pest

1. My father left me two cities,
one he took me to and one he kept a secret,
leaving it for his widow to give me, as she gave me
the check she said he'd meant to leave

although it was her check, and this is her city,
Buda-Pest. *And Buda-Pest*, I get a secret thrill in saying,
here on its Chain Bridge, *is more—Paris*
plus Magyars loving Paris!—Packing their trunks

full with Paris operas and grand magasins, smoking
back across the Alps in fur coats and hussar hats
a hundred twenty years ago, then unpacking broad boulevards—
Rakoczi, Andrassy ut—that Haussmann would know.

Walking here, did they—my father and his wife—
feel Paris underfoot? I do -- the Right Bank, Buda,
the Left Pest…but a strange, two-citied Paris,
the Germans' high Buda forest, the Serbs' low Pest

noisy with cars and buildings—two separate lands
Hungarians criss-cross as they do languages,
half a sentence German, the rest French, and a quick English gloss
for the visitor. I am faintly dizzy here, looking out

from a height at the two cities my father said he saw,
when he finally put it in his letters, as one cold,
pockmarked gulag, full of occupation's gray debris,
Nazi boots, Stalin's statue in Heroes Square, the Terror

before the Terror Museum—not Buda Castle
but a rivery dungeon cell his sister-in-law occupied
as an American spy. As an American, even in the Eighties' thaw,
he'd scuff his shoes, turn his collar up, pull on a hussar hat

for the walk to Pest for the Herald-Trib, smuggling it home
under his coat, hussar-hatted head down: no English
to tell on him. He hated it here, he wrote, tossing off
the secret visits as as meaningless as a meaningless affair,

tossing in the wife he married in secret (or at least in secret
from me) as simply an initial ("*I.*"); telling me only
to never go. My secret from him (though he is dust now
back in his beloved France)—I've come.

2. I stand above a river I want to make the Seine,
(to get the balance of a map I know) but which pulls me
east, whose rich brown swath proclaims broadly
it is no framed French photograph of a river, but the broad master vein

of a continent, carrying Bavaria to the Black Sea in seven languages,
every one strange to me, and the Danube no double
for anything. The Hungarians know that in Buda-Pest
their Duna, at her deepest, is home. They crown its crossing

with the bridge I cross, a grand chain between two towers—
the lion-hearted Szechenyi. Looking up, now, from the quay, I see also
what I am told Hungarians see, the past indelible behind every scene:
towers numb and empty-handed, sky blank, hyphen rent by war;
and then again the glittering string that makes this Buda-Pest.

3. Now *on* the river, in a sleek dinner boat about to sail, I see
my father's second wife, Ilona, arrive on the red-carpet gangplank
to a cheer, host at ninety of her own grande fête,
home on her own Danube. Glasses clink, crystal and champagne.

A gypsy band makes a dance Franz Liszt made parlor French
Ferenc's wild *verbunko* once again. Men in dinner jackets raise toasts
in seven languages: *Ilona!*—Ilona, who spans the century,
brings the feudal Hapsburg woods of childhood games

through two wars and a long iron siege down to this sunny July night,
a luminous chain. So much history, or champagne, a hundred
happy bubbling voices in a strange, orphan language, dizzies me.

What do I know? My father was loved here, in this dark city
he swore he hated, and never took me to; by a wife
I'm no relation to, but who I hold now, in my glass,
a bright jewel. Here darts a silent ghost

across a bridge we sail under. Here swirls past
a flotsam-bit of memory, trailing worn debris.
My father, who in his sentimental age grandly
left me Paris, and hid this foreign world—

a secret (like the secret father who would leave me
in Paris long ago)—has, malgré lui, left me
Buda-Pest, a city where no one forgets anything,
but no one needs to; and Ilona, my step-mother,

who is not just beautiful for ninety,
but simply beautiful. Tonight her laughter
is the cello and the violin. Why not laugh,

when laughter has such a range of notes?
The key is foreign, eastern, and old.
Tonight I get to love this as my own.

The Big Line

How could she carry it through,
create, on stage, the Liszt—
a building that she drew
through time, its shape entire
in the first, the second, every note?

Her brain and hands were large enough
to hold the lighted frame with room
for breath. The great sonata was the Abbé's church,
a structure made of stone, and glinting
roses, sun, and spires;
and in the left hand, cryptic saints—
the bottom chant, the ground, the bones.

The audience was silent as a tomb,
but moving there, at work, alive,
as the part each held, that crux,
became the pilgrim's way.

How then, Mother, did you play
your life without an arch, a spine?
A future, in your grasp, transformed?
Or did I come too late to see
the life that rose as big as any line
contained, in our years,
in your hands, your brain?

The Dark

"By voice, I mean style of thought…the sound of an authentic being."
—*Louise Gluck*

Voice is our other body, how we move in the dark.
From that point on, you rarely moved from where you sat,
watching strangers brightly, enduring it all,
the Echo scarf I'd helped you drape across your hollowed neck
a dash of post-operative chic.

How light your body seemed without its voice;
I found myself thinking my way into it,
trying out being without a voice. But it was the dark
I endured, I think, Mother, as we sat

mastering the new breathless argot,
I spooning too fast the thoughts I read
in the shape of your lips.
Sometimes you would simply close your mouth,
and watch me, as if I were deaf.

And I am. How silent it has been, forgotten
until now, when a line in a book takes me—
makes me close my eyes, and lays me
into that longing, the voice I reach for
so alive and moving toward me in the dark.

The Hidden Isle

After Arnold Böcklin's painting, Isle of the Dead,
and Claude Debussy's "L'isle Joyeuse"

"Joyeuse" was not the island on the wall
whose stories you told me, dreamy, turned
away from us to Böcklin's cliffs,

to towering trees you turned into family, a call
of love from those you'd lost and yearned
to find within their gates. I yearned also, as if

the painting told a deeper truth than all
the childish stories I had learned
in childish years. Rachmaninoff

was drawn there too, a pilgrim to the isle
of death. But for all you mourned,
Mother, days wound in grief,

I heard you late at night, while
you thought I slept—or you didn't care?—
at the piano with another isle, Debussy's motif

a love that lives, a hope, joyeuse. Of all
your secrets, I choose this, music bare
and breathing (not words, nor deathly art), to believe.

Fernande

A rough wool sweater in a trunk blossoms
into ancient flowers in winter—Fernande.
Who was she? The cook, governess, nurse

I abandoned when my parents abandoned
their marriage. The woman I forgot, taking up again
with my mother once home in the States.

The body of Paris always comes back in a scent:
the Metro, the courtyards, the steamy tabacs;
a long-packed sweater unfolding my Fernande,

the luxe Gallic bosom; thick arms
lifting me out of the smashed dinnerplates,
away from the two drunk Americans into the lap

of a Frenchwoman who had killed nine Germans
in one year, and seemed would kill for me.
I want to name something after her,

take the name I said carelessly
a hundred times a day, all the time asking
for something, *Fernande, je veux*

quelques chose à manger, Fernande,
je veux aller dehors—I want,
I want—I want Fernande's adult eyes

looking into mine; and to breathe
her womanly fragrance one more time;
and to say, I name this: Whatever part of me,

having traveled from an outer arrondissement
on a dark February morning, arrives on time,
and starts the kettles in the kitchen:
Fernande.

Fernande, whatever part of me is faithful.

The Payment

I loved my mother's death, the one and only
where I could do no wrong. (When she died
I was still a young woman, and she was old—sixty.)

You could almost say it was *my* death—
a daughter so entitled she could laugh
without that fear one always has around someone else's
mother's, father's, wife's, husband's, lover's death—

My own death, except I got to manage it,
and look good in the black dress. And laugh!
If I wanted to.

I am wistful, now, for such liberty, dressing today
carefully, for the death of my husband's brother's wife.
I compose my face, as is proper, for the formal hug,
but hushed by the raw, sudden sadness
of her young daughters' faces, their grief,
my composed words of comfort come out instead
a mad whisper from beyond:

Do with this what you will—It's yours.
This is what being a daughter means,
what you have paid for.

Finom

"Finom"—That's what you say in Hungary
about delicious soup. In my bowl,
the soup gleams Hapsburg yellow
flecked with rusty paprikash,
buttery with chicken and spaetzle.

I look up from my bowl and say it—
"fee-nome"—and Agnes the cook beams,
and my stepmother Ilona beams,
as if I had done something wonderful also.
The small apartment is all aroma now,

happy for us to breathe it. Am I drunk?
On the walls Ilona's pictures float:
a great stag slain beneath a steed from whom
the steely count faces us, swathed in bear and stoat—
Ilona's father no more dead than mine who stands

in mid-century American shirtsleeves next to a red Mustang
and faithful boxer Flick at a roadside stop
in the hills above Beirut, the city
where he and Ilona met; or than I, raising a glass
on the square in St-Jean-de-Luz, the sheen

on the warm Bordeaux catching like a camera obscura
my husband and the sea beyond in crystal miniature.
Now, this January day in Budapest, I fill myself
with what will warm me in my own allotted winters—
these fathers, sisters, husbands, brothers,

dogs, arrayed on walls and tables, all here
in one spell of soup for which there is a word
"finom," delicious in its bright upward kiss,
its Magyar gift. Here, a strange adjective
becomes an intimate noun,
a necessary name.

A Person

A whale is one, and an ape;
an elephant and a parrot,
in our modern, post-anthropocentric view.

In the last century, they weren't,
and neither was the woman
who pieced together jigsaw scenes

by the hour, picking up and putting down
her cigarette. When I came home
from school to find her dressed

not in a robe, but in her charcoal suit
and pumps, handbag packed, I knew
what adventure was in store. Climbing

into the car, slamming our doors,
off we drove to the Wisconsin Grill
where we ordered two hamburger steaks

sogging the white bread with their bloody juice,
and a Coke for me, and for her a drink
that she would lift slowly, swirl

the gin and vermouth, and sip from a long thirst.
I knew what she'd say, a sentence
I think of now, when those who swim,

lumber, or fly are said to be
what she only wanted to feel like
at four o'clock, on certain secret afternoons.

Lost & Found

We take it in stride, the New Normal
(where a forty-year absence material-
izes out of the cloudy goo-
gle and we snap the handy trope,
friending the old friend,
xchanging email catch-up on
a lifetime in breezy Xmas letters only
xtra long by a 'graph or two), as if this weren't

A miracle bodying forth, that you—*my* you
(and you, and you) so lost, deep in the heart-
hollow, abiding in the silent dream
where every forgotten friend lives—
Live! *Have* lived, and now have leaned
your parallel universe my way,
allowing my hands purchase,
the palpable joy of our embrace,
at only the cost of knowing, again,
who is equally real, and so really lost.

THE TRUTH OF ART

The Short Hop

for Luis Aparicio

Once, not to startle and fend,
but to step into it,
glove down on the ground,
grace meeting fear and knowledge
in one catch!

Ars Poetica

"I learned to talk from my mother," I said,
and was startled: Doesn't everyone?
But "learned from"—
as if it were playing the piano,
or making the sylsalat at Christmas?
But it was: Her speech,
invented for me, her patience
letting my mouth and tongue
work the vowels, open
and open, then clench consonants
hard in my teeth, all nibbled edge,
and me still making of it a gibberish,
a babble; a glottal soup,
a drool;

My answering nothing but a rhythmic rumination
of nonsense syllables. But she kept on,
now a whisper, now a song, and in a while
the words became words: *Epitome*
and *punctilio, modicum*
and *masterly*; plenty of slang
like *vamoose* and *delish*, and play
in the "*Ditto*" that either one
could say, and smile (our secret).

This language of the days
of our small world, dangled from,
rolled in, colored and toddled,
and finally slept on, a pillow,
the sun,

Is now so many vocabularies ago, fields
of cultivated speech—

But with this odd sentence I remember
what came first,
the ravishing world she made
me take, word by hungry word,
and how much more there is to tell
in our original language.

March Ladybugs

The window frames the white landscape
flat as a page above my desk.
I look, as if to contemplate the end of winter—
the stream's first froth breaking through the ice,
the cedar pillars pinioning the sky.
Another March, another nature scene I'm baffled by.

Out of the blue, the tribe silently enters,
a hunched migration marching placidly across the snow—
Ladybugs, rescuing blank beauty with a scrawl of life.
Now, mornings, I watch them in their earnest journeys
edge to edge, and back again. One cluster cuts away
for treetops, another swoops headlong into the brook's March flow.

I watch them for a week, their boxed-in wanderings
companionable, until the morning when new warmth
sends them scuttling, sun-driven, for the sky. Suddenly they turn,
wild, into the room, a flock of winged and monstrous Huns—
and as soon subside—again the tiny, patient nuns
I know, though my heart still pounds.

And then, today, it's done. To a lady,
they've let go the landscape for the page,
littering the foolscap in a dying chatter.
In the box above, it's spring, but flat.
Together for the week when winter
turned into another season, my bugs

And I went nowhere, and only a child
would bury them, or try to read letters

in their spotted shells, or words
(like "sorrow") in the way they fell.

Guess Work, Scientists, Poets, and Bees

For a high school physics class studying the relationship between science & poetry

It comes seemingly out of the blue
for both of them—poet's metaphor, scientist's guess—
the chance that may resonate
in mathematics, or in observation.

Take Newton's sizzling leap—apple,
moon—the line of force between
as suddenly straight as the moon's
curving path, as true as *What if*

circling's just another way to fall,
to go straight ahead in two directions,
all the time forever?

Imagine this: A topsy-turvy world
where Fall begins the year,
and commencement is the end;

Where we're commended to be fruitful
when the light's most thin, and quit
when trees have just begun to leaf—

In this world, paradox-riddled at the core,
would Keats' bees—ahum
in lazy, busy summer work
at autumn flowers—be wrong

to think warm days will never cease?
Would we, to join them—and the scientist
and poet—in the pleasure

of a world where work is play,

and the bright guess (secret ratio) reveals
what we ought to take the measure of?

After all, it's not the moon alone
that we shall never see the same
since Newton's guess, but the apple

itself, forever changed in its bright Fall
roundness, by Calculus
as much as by the cider-press.

Falling In Love with the Octopus

Down I went,
headlong. Why him?
He wasn't the smart one, the one who perched
like a giant insect on the tank wall and eyed the glass jar
only a split-second before one big snakey arm
struck, scooping it up, another lassoed the lid,
and a third (still plenty to spare) clawed out the hapless crab
and tossed it down the soft but beakish mouth like popcorn.
So an octopus is a problem solver—So what?
So is a crow. So, some say, are certain bugs.
We might as well concede the whole animal kingdom
on that score. What got me was something less,
and more. All the while Mr. Smarty Pants was clocking through
his fancy mason jar routine, in the next tank my guy—
you might have thought he'd poke a tentacle or two
at his own jar, or just bobble around like a lollygag cephalopod,
but instead—he watched. Hung five (and drifted three)
on his own tank wall, then with his ugly, alien eyes—
now I was watching, something inside me on its own
tenterhooks—followed the action next door step by step.
Then he took a breath (or was that me?), dropped down
like Spiderman and sauntered (in his ugly, eight-armed, alien way)
over to his own glass jar. You can guess the rest.
Someone else might have taken notes, thought her way through
to a conclusion befitting our sapient species. Not me.
My brain went under, no more use than the pea-brain
of some lowly mollusk. All I saw was the ocean,
all the leagues and years of it, all the ugly, lumbering life of it.
Oh, the old gray sponge flung out an arm or two,

grasping at one idea or another like lifelines—restaurants
with dipping sauce; some snappy metaphor; new legislation; God—
but then with a burp flopped belly up and sank;

Leaving only my heart to take this in, grow full with it,
in my chest hang saclike and inky with it, four chambers
blossoming to eight, vena cava and aorta and whatever else comes in,
    and out—
now ancient vessels, now swimming for deep water.

The Secret Hand

Those years, a secret hand
seemed to be stocking the shelves just ahead of me.
Every used bookstore had at least two of the three books
I ritually looked for—downtown in Portland,

in Seattle by the fishmarket, in a seedy part of Denver—
the white script, orange jacket, familiar heft,
exactly where expected. These were the books
I ritually gave away, could keep giving

a new friend, an old lover, someone I admired—
giving anyone my last copy, without a qualm.
I could give it all away!

Remembering those years, you remember your voice—
limber, jangling the door, striding straight back,
certain: Now down on all fours
to pry out *The Life of Poetry*,
now lithely braced against the laddertop
for Levertov's *Poet in the World* leaning into your grasp.

Who knows when it changes, when Kinnell
is hard by Li-Young-Li, and the friendly clerk
doesn't think *The Poet in the World*
is something she has ever heard of?
Had you held on too long to the last
Life of Poetry? Was that even the name?

Admit it. You never really got whatever Rukeyser
was saying—still, it seemed so rich, so like something

you were made to love, and everyone you gave it to seemed grateful.
Perhaps if you had kept on with your French,
managed to get through Piers Ploughman, properly
    appreciated Shakespeare.
You were always going to.

That itinerant God—*my* itinerant God—
making the eternal rounds of the bookshops,
digging the same three books out of His knapsack—
wanting me to find them—is through.

Whether the secret hand
really shelved them
is as moot as childhood trauma.
I thought it did.

And now—
If what I want is books,
there's the Internet,
the whole searchable world.

What to make of it—Being blessed,
intended—or simply here?
The door, the bell, a voice that stops
at the front desk to ask directions,
the random shelves—
the musty smell of possibility still quickens.
Maybe—why not? Rumi—maybe Dana Gioia,
or something in translation—
What is here, although reduced,
is infinite.

Tuckerman: The Line

Frederick Goddard Tuckerman, 1821-1873, American poet
Witter Bynner, 1881-1968, American poet

Tuckerman was Bynner's Bynner, his decade deep
in another time. I find
Bynner finding him, the reading mind
and the writing, by one candle. The page keeps
a sitting room, a wood. The line leaps
again. That century is far,
but the same day, the very hour—
a circle on each solitary leaf.

Tuckerman is minor, some sonnets and an odd line,
but in it, Bynner's joy, and mine.
His hands hold tender, inconsolable loss in a way that says
it is not only his.   Oh Bynner—may I call you Bynner?—what
    breaks at my eyes:
not the steep sun, nor wind, but the mind that reckoned
this line, the beat of knowing.   And the finding second!

The Editor

She is sixty, red-haired, funny.
She uses pencils,
sometimes an old Kaypro
and in the last stage, she smokes.
She works at the dining-room table
in the house overlooking the ocean,
in a second career she can afford
after long service as executive secretary
to the company founder, who some say she slept with.

But she is not a muse, and views the wreck
with a curious eye, cool.
"What have we here?" she says.
Your answer is a curse. You croak.

No matter. She has her work:
Sets down your page, copies out the final lines
in a brisk but flowing hand, and where the tiny comma dug
its fingernails into hapless crumble,
she sweeps a lavish dash
that heralds the arriving city
suddenly standing in your own longhand.

One Good New Poem

is all you need
to get back
in. Strike
any bargain He likes—
your immortal soul
is no use like this anyway.

But stake you
to
  one
  good
  new
  poem,
and before the night is out, you'll be back here
with sonnets, sestinas, ballads, pan-
toums, *armies* of heroic lines
that will win back   *anything.*
You can do it, with
one—

    Nothing.
    Nothing.

This is winter, that light pressed
under glass, that preserved memory
of light, your heart
as still and small as the tiny winter day,
  as the days that stand
    still.

You'll buy a gun!   Hold up
Sharon Olds or Christopher What's-His-Name:
Give me that
poem you don't
need it.

Or children! Children have poems
coming out of their ears.
You'll take an entire 3rd grade
hostage, make them do those
dream exercises; scoop up buckets
of images they'll never miss,
the little bastards.

   Oh God, these are children's poems
   and Sharon's voice, and what's-his-name's
   name, and here you are with

Nothing.
Nothing.
If the damned *light*
weren't in a vice, if the night
that's come so early and stayed
so late would let up—

   No. OK.
   OK, then *try.*
   Try *harder.*
   Scratch out
   half a stanza,
   stick with it.

Part Two

          —Loose! Yes, out of the leaden echo,
the golden. This resonance can't be accidental
(Did you know Hopkins, that one, was Liz and Richard's favorite,
didn't you always imagine them saying it to each other in bed,
in silk, drunk with poetry and their own accents, didn't it make it
hard to understand what went wrong for them?)
when there could be all this
life, this color, this heart finally in the still
unforcing, in the slight slide of light deeper across
one day, still winter but February's sleight of hand
with the seasons, how could you doubt (But you didn't imagine
the newsreels on the tarmac, Liz alone, fat again, waving off
reporters, cut to Richard flicking off a cigarette
as he too hurries to an airport door, the black and white
proof that luxury of words, and of loving words,
wasn't, isn't, enough) that resonance—
echoes—might come
from ground still cold,
or cold again.
Didn't you always imagine?

The Truth of Art

Brushed, bathed, awake for my turn: She's ready now.
Airplane notes in hand, I'm ready too:
Thank you. Remember—? Goodbye.
(They say the dying want the truth.)

The truth is, I drop my notes at what I see: Pam's head
a wobbly baby twice its normal size, yet her voice warms my name
as always. The host she always was brushes the sheets smooth,
the bed her foyer and the door flung wide.

Down the hall friends fuss and bustle, a resolute machine
that knows the drill: Brew soup, blend green and yeasty drinks,
assign an arsenal of pills to clockwork bins. Deliveries arrive,
and airport runs are made. The wheels of compassion turn.

But in here, Pam's in charge, brushing an old photo album aside
and announcing what's next: A Fall show of new work,
a party we'll all come back for. And as for the past, she's done:
Done with the great burnt vistas and the giant rocks,

Done with the Delta dirt your hands could feel, the smell;
My God, done with representation entirely!
Has she forgotten how we loved this work,
the grand canvasses more the place than the place itself?

Yes. She has the new thing in her eye: Pure color,
the seeing through to paint laid bare of everything
but hue—Color, until the colors pop!
Outside I hear "It's time," and I can see

That time and drugs have worked their well-known wreck,
ballooned one leg and arm, and turned a beauty's face into a puff—
But Pam's clear gaze has drawn me in to where she stands
in her studio, primed for work; a pleasure to watch

In her splattered shirt, sleeves rolled; a pleasure to see
holding once more the full brush (the brush
with its own appetite for something new, its tongue
of rich desire: *To make the colors pop.*)

Those magic weekends when the contra-dance
old friends do together after months or years
came round to Pam and me the ones side-by-side,
chopping vegetables or hiking up the trail, our turns to talk

Often stuttered, Pam's legendary warmth no less real
for holding an inwardness that I trod lightly on—
but then we'd get to Art, our own solitary cells...
our projects, impersonal and in our bones.

If the dying want the truth, I'd say
"to make the colors pop" unsettles me, this turn
to the loud, this frivolity (not *deliquesce*? not *sing*?)
but the woman wanted to do new work.

And Pam, the truth is, so do I.

Do You Play American Music?

Thanks to President Give 'em Hell Harry having sworn
he'd punch his nose and other body parts for the review
that said Margaret, darling First Child, couldn't sing,
the music critic was famous that year.

I, meanwhile, was a nobody, a seven-year-old
stashed glumly on a metal chair
in the back of a high-ceilinged studio,
waiting out each Tuesday afternoon, nose
in a comic book, ears closed to the old teacher in front
(a blind bear banging his cane "faster"),
and to the Prokofiev my mother was learning for a comeback—

which she had, the East Garden Court
packed, all bustling coats and scrapes of chairs,
then silent for the calm destruction
of everything they knew about music;
then on their feet with cheers.

The next day in the Post, the critic cheered too,
but at the end had to nail the unspoken oath
with a raised eyebrow at the Russian repertoire:
"Mrs. Weisert, do you play American music?"
…Anyone can see 1952 was not the year

to throw a bright red flag of a sonata into the airwaves
of our nation's capital where Margaret had so recently sung
"God Bless America" in Constitution (DAR) Hall
under the beaming gaze of those other, gray-haired daughters
of the you know what, which along with God was then in full cry,

but my mother's choice wasn't—I think wasn't—so much
courage, or a political point (her fellow-traveler years
long past), but the simple fact: that year, this work
was the hardest, newest thing in town,
and goddammit Prokofiev was hers.

And mine? At the radio's opening shot
my heart takes off, knowing the charge of notes
whole, and the bursting charge that's next, riding
the sweep across the steppes, the blizzard fugue;
wrapped tight around it straight through to the breathless end

when I look up—now from the New York Times—
look hard, past a comic book, teacher's cane,
and metal chair; past HUAC and hearings;
past the last days of the Truman years,
and careful what you say, who you tell, what you—

to a woman in a piano studio starting over
every Tuesday, damp, out of breath
on the thirtieth, the fiftieth run, oblivious
to the dark times, and even to her child
learning something, that year, about art.

Imagination Itself

To the eyes of the man of imagination,
Nature is imagination itself.
—William Blake

Who needs half a million unpronounceable forms of life
Half a world away? Ah, you do, they say,
and enumerate the ways:

Glues, dyes, inks,
Peanuts, melons, tea,
Golf balls, paint, and gum,
Mung beans, lemons, rice,
And a fourth of all the medicines you take,
And a fifth of all the oxygen you breathe,
And countless life-prolonging secrets their wild cousins know
to tell the Iowa corn and the garden tomato.
And if that's not enough, think of rubber—
and where we'd all be, rattling down the Interstate
on wooden wheels.

And that's only the stuff we know how to use,
And that's only the half-million species we know how to name.

And in the time it took to say this
Five thousand acres more are gone.
And by the time that this year's kindergarten class
is thirty-five, most of what is now alive—

But wait. What if—What if this deluge of mind-boggling
statistical connectedness were, true as it is,
only the least of it? What if the real necessity
were of another kind, the connection

Not with what you consume, or do, but who you are?

With your own imagination, the necessity there
of places that have not been cleared to till,
of the luxury of all that buzzing in the deep,
of a glimpse of feather or translucent insect wing
a color that's so new it tells you light and sound
are, indeed, just matters of degree, and makes your vision hum

And makes you think the universe could hum
in something like the wild, teeming equilibrium
of the rain forest.

SKYLARK

Grandfather, Balloon

How Deep Is the Ocean

A balloon in a jazz room is odd, especially one
not festively skimming the ceiling but resting
like a big cartoon baby on the table, bobbing slightly
in front of an old man who sits waiting
for the first notes of a Berlin ballad
he once heard Lee Wiley sing. Tonight,
the singer is his granddaughter, and he's deaf.

But as a word "grandfather" surely holds a child, and play,
as much as age and dignity, so why shouldn't the old man
hold this red balloon, light and smiling?
He tips his head to it
when Alexis starts to sing, lifts his fingers
so they barely graze the skin, and from then on
his smile and nodding head are right in time.

I know the song's question wasn't meant for a reply
(those depths its marvel), but I think we are seeing it
in what travels from the stage to this table,
from one shore to another, from the young singer
to the grandfather holding a child's toy and hearing
the waves as they arrive on the skin of a balloon
into the skin of his hands, into a song about love.

Arriving at Molly and Mike's to the Music of Harold Arlen

As if they always had it on—
as if "Don't know why/there's no sun
up in the sky" were the theme
for everything they make here,

Molly and Mike in their shipshape condo
floating high above Toronto and the lake,
in these four walls: a place
as deftly packed as a poem,

as clean and compact a craft,
imagination's triumph over mere square feet.
Mike's study is a narrow strip the length
of the apartment, a starboard cabin crowded

as a Dublin bar with words and argument,
yet silent as a church. The mild man
comes out to shake my hand, welcome me
almost with a bow, then returns

to close reading's wild vocabulary.
In front, Molly's study is a glass lookout
on the vast Ontario blue, our United States
way out on the horizon—

                        They don't,

of course; I doubt that Arlen's dreams
are the theme at #1041
except today, for my arrival,
the stranger known through words alone.

My vertigo steadies in the drink
Molly hands me, in the toast we raise
to all that words can recognize, to a kind
of friendship. To the warmth
of Arlen's stormy weather. To the magic,
many ways of art, and kindness.

Antonio Carlos Jobim

I would love to have called him "Tom",
because someplace in every song he wrote I heard my name,
but since he will not come to New York again,
and anyway would not recognize me
on the street wearing this poor translation,
I will try to know your name,
listening as lovers listen to Jobim,
forming my lips in the unfamiliar language.

Dancing with Shirley Horn

You don't actually move,
but you do dance, you know
you are dancing by the way
your arms open, and your knees
do what they do in a swoon;
but you don't drop, you stand
quite still; it's all
within, the salt water river
washing you inside
like a cat's tongue, and you let
the cat, and the arms, and the knees
all join the dance, and you—
you close your eyes and let the sweet salt flow.

For Harold Arlen

I know, I let Gershwin kiss me
in a restaurant on 49th Street.
How could I help it when he was writing
"I Loves You Porgy" for me, right there
as I cut my steak and raised a bite
to my mouth, coming up behind me
and lingering on my shoulder, unbuttoning
whatever I was wearing, so there was
nothing between me and the song but my skin?

And that time with Rodgers
in the apartment on West 93rd—
I loved it, loved the way he promised
to remember everything, every inch
a kind of vow—December does that to me,
the warmth of a piano in winter.
I see now how it was theater music,
how the B-flat in the second measure was sugar,
the A-flat in the third much too beautiful,
but then? Then it was nothing but beauty.

I suppose if anyone would understand
it would be you…

And it's really never anyone
but you, all you need to do is walk in the door
and that E-flat halfnote will stop the conversation.
Just stand there and I'll drop everything,
tell my friends the night is over, go home.

Just lean in the doorway while I walk around
the table putting out every candle, maybe taking
a final glance in the mirror before dousing the last
at a face older than I remembered—has it been
that long?—but you only smile, hands in your pockets,
the notes blue enough to forgive a lifetime,
the drop from A to low C a look I thought
I'd never see again, the certain look of you
reminding me
this could be our shining hour.

The Man That Got Away

Two AM in LA, moony waves of neon and bougainvillea
Norman Maine wades through, hopeful and boyish—
entering the club like a child tiptoeing downstairs,
taking a seat at a dark back table to wait for something wonderful

which he gets: The sidemen come to life in a blue pool of light
up front, the blue hour when they play for themselves alone
(and a middle-aged boy in the shadows). The young woman—
still Esther in this early part—tosses her guys a look,

a big shrug that takes the world with it,
and then proceeds to show how in a prim blue dress
you can sing like a naked animal. We'd cringe
at how she flings the song everywhere, the walls, floor,

ceiling, except we've been waiting too. When the music stops,
and she returns like a Sufi or a medium, clothed and dazed
and laughing, we go to her with him, take her arm, march her
out to the night and, gripping her small shoulders,

try to explain what she's done. Norman thinks it's art,
or star presence, but as I play the tape for my latest lover,
I think it's not what she's done, but what we want.
I've pressed the button on this scene of mid-last-century

rapture a dozen or two times, know the rank black undertow
it drags, pure Hollywood; the ripe misogyny embracing its cargo
like seaweed; but this is the first reel, my lover
is as new as Esther, and I am as young
as the middle-aged man whose eyes were shining in the dark.

Another NPR Report

An iPod playlist
of songs from one's youth,
has been shown to rouse
the Alzheimer brain to sing,
and dance—connect.

A kind of miracle.
We'll need a miracle,
 the twenty-five
or is it fifty percent of us
going that way…

Though isn't the news
something we've long known
every year we gathered at the beach,
lining up one more time
for Chain of Fools?

Didn't those chords all at once
undiminish us, bring us back, whole,
to a kind of love we can only
stomp to, shout, wave? Shake on
our fine rags of memory?

Oh, imagine: Everything gone,
utterly lost, dead weight on a nation
(you think we don't care?)—A visitor

is kind, fixes the earbuds, presses Play,
and one more time, we rise,

we know.

Skylark

You have to envy their vocabulary, the jazzmen,
the hundred-odd words they all know
in any language—Swedish, French.

All they have to do is say a name—
for example, "Skylark"—and they are free
of the ordinary necessities:

That this is a bird, or that it is not,
or that it ever was. In this language,
what things are takes time, rooms,

Voices sounding out each source
and then taking the turn, a break
taking off who knows where—

Leaving me, frankly,
lost,
floating in a dark and smoky room, lost—

As I am, lately, in love,
certain once again that this is too far gone,
nothing to catch, to follow—

Lost, and yet if no longer listening,
not entirely having stopped waiting—
a kind of listening?—so that when the two

Simple notes begin their return—
the slightest shadow beyond abstract chords
now scattering—and wholly changed sing clear,

I am arriving too,
fresh as if from aloft,
having heard everything.

AWAY

Heroics

for Joko

Certainly not mine, nor
the life-saving ones
I don't sign up for,

but the ragged, extra measures
the poems take to make
their way beyond me.

The Persistence of Roses

White roses of Kleenex pleated and held
by bobby pins, their leaves fanned out in petals
flowered on the cafeteria table around me.
A hundred other kids bore down profoundly
on the Great Big Test whose results would mark
our lives. I'd finished half an hour ago, a lark,
and waited, bored, for the sweating lot. Me,
alone in a ring of roses. Outside: the not-me.

Now, outside this waiting room are people in clothes,
but here we're all in filmy gowns, pink and roses.
A girl, a young mother, an old broad, and me.
The girl's eyes are more afraid, and so we
others are all mothers.   The marks will be
different, each dear body, or the same—our "tests".
But there are lives of roses in our breasts,
calm waiting past the ring of me and not me.

The Bra

Pas moi—
bourgeois,
ignored
(drawer-stored)
for years
appears
all at once buoyant on top of the underpants
asking to be worn—the old significance
embraced. Voilà—a hug
of lace, elastic tug
and I'm a college girl dressing for a date.
You never felt natural, old bra, but late
on a Saturday night, what would the thrill
have been without the boyish grapple—then the "Ah…"

Soon we'll go our separate ways, having had our fill
of one another—but tonight we'll celebrate that first hurrah.

Erasure

I wake from dreams and call for Mommy—Call
for who she was when I was only small
and Mother hadn't brought her chill, the cig-
arette that kept me at arm's length. I call
again and through the spindled bars I see
the door is open, someone comes for me—
She'll take me from this dream, she'll hold me tight
and settle in the chair and stay the night
with arms I settle into, into rest—
forgotten wanting—and the only breast
I need, its rise and fall erasing time.
I breathe along, and, soon, my breathing slows,
for all I need to know, I know: I've called
her name and she came back to me. We hum
together, safe again, my mommy, me—

Mercy

My chest's a knothole and my arm's a stick.
I creak and sigh like something on a hill.
No—that's my right side, left is human still—
So—I'm half tree, half me; half well, half sick.

What was it Daphne did? Did I do half?
It wasn't love I ran from—yet the birds
I watch approach me almost seem to laugh
as if they knew the lies I've told, the words

I always thought I meant.   Ah—the human
side keeps digging, searching for a curse,
or something in the life, the shadow looming
in a thousand craven acts.   "Have mercy,"

says the tree, as if it knew this hill
is not a judgment, but a place to rest;
as if two mismatched halves could make me whole,
and sun and rain and earth could make me blessed.

The Images

i.
You think you can look inside yourself,
a talent discovered in high school
like the other easy gifts—fast wit,
pithy sentences, the best answers.

The x-rays inside the envelope
prove how wrong this is: picture
after picture of what I never saw—
and now, what isn't there,

like the Diana Court in *Lost Chicago*.
Why do I keep such images? They have nothing
to dreamily regard, no ocean-liner mezzanine
where I played hide-and-seek behind a stainless pier,
and they're ugly (not beautiful like Diana
shining in her fountain below), or they felt ugly when taken...

ii.
...As, laid out, I listened to what was developing
into my life. "Yes, there it is—
the possum shape, the teeth."
I answer something witty, a new class
to excel in, the better not to see
the creature suckling in the dark.

You think you can look inside yourself
and see what you're made of.

These days I can:

patched rag of flesh, my new flag;
sleek steel huntress, prow at the horizon;
and the lapping waves of an ocean
that can't be imagined
already being light, and nothing but light.

Away

Where the nipple was is air; what's left
a ribby floor that life's receded from—
and so has touch. And now, its mate's gone deaf,
dumbfounded. Practiced fingers feel like thumbs.

What a nipple does is concentrate
a cloud of fireflies into a flame
of light, or from one point elaborate
the hidden filigree. But "does" is not the same

as what the nipple was—not flesh alone
but all that flesh had learned: The warm frisson
before a touch; the lush suspense of thought
circling—the edge soft, the air taut.

So hold your hand away, and let me feel
it draw me, as it draws its silent wheel.

Love

Shouldn't love mean more to me by now?
Or at least, shouldn't something of the swell,
the waves of youth remain an undercurrent, chains
I could sing in, a warm, returning tide?

Couldn't I use the warmth in this cold time?
But it's me that's cold, that's lost
desire's home. I'd like to say love failed,
but it was me, here at my outpost,

where what I cry for is the singer
who stepped out of a hotel window despite
knowing the meaning in the songs as well
as Wilder, as well as anyone; where what moves
me is the distant human loss, and not
the man beside me, nor my own clenched need.

As If

Who am I
kidding? It's not all
roses, or words that rhyme.
It hurts. And then there's time
(no metaphor). Yet transform-
ation can not only soothe;
what rises out of form
can be the truth,

Or can be made (not "meant") to be.
No, rhymes don't make a "reason,"
and what the universe might tell, it can't be bothered telling me.

I am one woman in one turning season,
a Spring that returns "recurrence" to its root:
one unrepeatable day, alive and absolute.

WHERE WE WERE AND WHAT WE WERE DOING

Where We Were and What We Were Doing

August 19, 2003

In traffic, changing stations, sick of the news
where a woman with a rich European contralto
commemorates her friends, their great hearts
and their souls at this moment departing.

We had our own years of where-we-were
and what-we-were-doing, do we need these?
What are we supposed to do, having marched, and cooked
the great casseroles from the Women's Strike for Peace Cookbook,

and hosted the night meetings in our living rooms?
(Remember the talk, the certainty of where we were going?) Quaint,
that Apocalypse, its one-by-one bullets, its rapturous End.

*****

Late—but no end. The act of remembering is again
our stand, again our pledge…
But is it what the souls at that moment
would ask for, would want? Would it comfort
the passengers to know we would stop in our fields

And turn our eyes upward, and speak?

The News Photographers

for Chris Hondros and Tim Hetherington, April, 2011

About suffering they were never wrong,
the Old Masters, and the young and not so young
photographers are not either, taking pictures
in Biblical lands of Old Testament scenes
wired home for our breakfast,

the photographs as old and luminous
as paintings, the figures sacred
and brushed in oil.
Here a prophet raises a broken child
like a lamb to be laid on a rock,

here a father stands forsaken by God,
his eyes on ours; and there behind,
a fading smear of camo and a white face.
Out of our range, a cool professional
kneels in dust to hold the frame still,

click after click—the human position
in Gaza, Libya, Afghanistan. Taking in the beauty,
the Rembrandt shades, I am ashamed
to be seeing this as art, values
of light and dark, massed shapes, tones.

But it is art, and what Auden commends--
the timeless truth the masters understood--
our photographers know too:
their work is a picture in a newspaper,

a day we cannot help but turn away from

when the next day comes.
But they know more, our artists
of the camera—they must,
when it is they who see,
framing this world in their hands,
and they, as well, who fall.

Finding Wilfred Owen Again

Our college love affair was doomed
like all the romance I outgrew at twenty;
trench warfare's mad embrace be damned
along with Buffy Sainte-Marie and Nietzsche.
        And anyway, the war in Vietnam was ending.

For decades he lay silent in a book,
moved from Brooklyn to St Louis and LA
with curling snapshots, silver rings turned black,
the mildewed albums I will never play.
        I left him to his war; our war had ended—

Until I call, the offhand way you do old flames
(as if you hadn't kept their trail of numbers)
when something big has changed, or Armageddon looms.
(Shamed moment: Was it Rupert I remembered?
Romance imagined?)   Not now: War has descended—

distant and mine. I'm dazed, feckless, as lost
as my lost country. So I come here,
to find myself standing on shattered ground he blessed
with full eyes ninety years ago and hear
        him tell another time how war must end

in this fell field, on this dark page. The night
opens, closes, opens, a swinging sulphur rhythm in the flare
igniting each line end, the faces lit
and then eclipsed,
but always bright the names.

Dice with the Universe

Not our God: No chance
the people running
from the laws of physics
writ large on the rising
wall behind them will hear
the roar of a rolling
wave that once set
in motion could break
any other way.

"Resist Regret"

Injunction given in a seminar by the philosopher Sara Ruddick (1935—2011)

Reclining on the daybed, glass of wine
in one hand, the other hand fondling your neck,
Regret is the old lover you return to,

the one who knows who you were.
How you long to lie back, embrace
that perfect body, that Olympian mind,

the dizzying waste—Betray
the aging stranger you live with
who barely understands you,
but has your breakfast ready.

A Wonderful Life

for Mona

Once a year, we settled in to our Tennessee complaints,
sidelines to our husbands' games of badminton and hearts:
The aisles of Wal-Mart something Munch might paint,
our urbane souls smothered in the shopping carts.

And when your old Toyota, plump with pillows, fat-free snacks,
and family, receded at week's end through dusty clatter
into the August haze, your relieved wave a speck,
I'd breathe my own relief, fatigued with summer chatter,

and eager to get out myself, catch the morning plane
away from the brothers' cherished Home Place; ditch
the dung-strung walks, the dinner talk as stolid as the drains,
shed our once-a-year bond, the conspiratorial bitching

of sisters-in-law… Free until the next gathering of the fold
for some ritual obligation. But the next gathering is now, your
funeral, where I, expecting ritual grief, instead behold
you, a woman. My co-conspirator is a mere walk-on in the story

that today enlarges this congregation. What is this *fierce heart*,
this *fearless love*, this *force*,
that I so blindly—But regret oddly has no part
in this. The door swings, my oblivion a sudden source

of joy—like the stumbling into metaphor
not of one's own making: Glorious. The life
you held for those you loved, today an open door
for any poor soul stumbling in, breathes here, life to life.

Wake-Robin Trillium

First the leaves, showy as a tricorn hat
Miss Moore could fly in, then three
small sepals like a fairy hand

offering the tripetalous velvet flower,
its deep red a secret revealed
in one day's dawn—Trillium!

Only a wildflower, but each whorled tier
a precise one-third turn from the last,
the fugue of three as clockwork as Bach.

A lifetime, and I never saw them;
Now I see them everywhere
rising out of early May colt's foot,

unruly schools of trout lily,
every morning perfect
with their discovery.

Until the day Trillium dips its proud head
as if in modesty, trembles
and blows away. The great leaves

return to the green crowd
on the forest floor,
and my awakening to the spell

of Trillium seems as mad and lost
as the love that held me trembling

a lifetime ago, as the wild willingness to yield

everything to beauty, let go the year-round,
earthbound human life and be
the robin who comes alive
once a year at a flower's call.

In Sasebo, Nagasaki

Don't ask, don't tell

I am trying to describe a simple news story,
what I read about the Belleau Wood,
not the crime but what came before the crime.
I am trying to tell my friends
what is important about this ship
that would later be known for one sailor,
ashore, beaten by his shipmates—and nothing
betrays me there, I can say that part, page one,
easily, even the horror of a phrase
never meant to be anything but a cliché,
now literal—*"to a pulp"*—for his crime;

My friends know that story, but what I want
to tell them is this other part, the buried news:
how the ship was dark, rough trade feared in every port,
so that when it turned for Sasebo
scores of fishermen set out in boats to say,
Go back! Go back!, and another sailor,
smelling the dark musk, helicoptered out
in time. But my voice, never meant
to be literal, but a modulation,
instead just breaks
and pours out the truth. The ship
is in my chest, still at sea,
and the dozens of tiny oars are beating there,
and I am the one crying
"Go back! Go back!"

The Best Funeral Ever

Why doesn't everyone think of this? His daughter
is a minister herself, perhaps that gives her license;
perhaps it's the art he loved, or just the indelible

imprint of a person on the people who love him.
Perhaps it's love. At first, we are taken aback,
seeing what she's laid out—not a body, out here in the park,

and not the standard photographs or video montage,
but his actual clothes—the giant jacket hung
from a branch on a tree, and on the ground

his shoes, huge now without the tall man to stand
in them. Ellie stands on the grassy rise, and instead of
talking about him, remembering this and that,

she gives us Dan's arms, hands splayed out
in his wide gesture of amazement, voice lifting
from a charged hush to an onrush of words

for the latest earth-shaking idea, invention—his, yours,
some genius across the world. Isn't there a rule
that says you don't mimic the dead? Don't bring

a dead man's shoes to his funeral? But a daughter
can make her own rules. Ellie is all he used to
bend our ear about, and this is the best

funeral ever. We don't learn anything, we just see
what we didn't even know we'd noticed.
For an hour, we grow big, amazed; like Dan.

The Beautiful Boys

What I saw then
(I a woman on the sidelines),
those Mondays, dark at the Public Theater,
in the vaulted lobby where you gathered
from your offices, threw back your ties,
and drew the house into something electric—
an arc, a grand line—theater!—

"I Will Survive" not yet an anthem;
what I saw as you spun, fell
in love, all of you, dark or blonde,
alabaster or dusk; smooth, muscled,
groomed; crisp Oxford an Ivy League
Harvard would have died for.

Even from the sidelines, how could I not
want to touch your shining hair, catch
your shining eyes? Swoon at the knees
with the toss of your heads? Catch my heart
seeing what you saw?

Who am I to memorialize you,
I, a woman who has reached an age
that you would never entertain,
and in such a distant world?

But I lived in the City
when the City was alive with you,
and I am drawn to see what I saw then:
Your youth as it flew, its beat

a beat we all caught, a beauty
that reached us all, sidelines be damned—

Drawn, from the new world I live in,
to reach back, to ask—
What would *you* make of this world, now?
You, who made art out of so many dark nights?
To imagine (a watcher, a listener still)
that I may overhear—

      For starters, "Equality"?
      A hoot, n'est-ce pas?
      You'd chintz it up,
      paper the kitchen in roses,
      set a very large Lab
      by the fire: *Mes amis,*
      voila, "Le mariage!"

      Or a cocktail, without
      a pretty twist, a jewel hue,
      a kick? *Mais c'est*
      incroyable!
      You'd buy a round
      for the house, raise a wry
      toast to Burroughs Wellcome
      stock. You'd
      drain the cup.

…*For the cup*—

What I am asking, really, is would you,
then, cross with me into our age?

But who am I to reach, to yearn, to say,
imagining you
in all of your beautiful manhood,
you are my boys?

The Year of Reading Yeats

My friend went back to reading Yeats the year
she went back to the farm, claiming the land
as land, leaving a smart, well-dressed career
for dirt. This was her home. She'd planned
how what had grown tobacco now would bear
(a mile below where grinding, snorting bands
of bulldozers pawed the earth and air grew thick)
the fruit suburbanites would pay to pick.

Her father planned it too—their dream. The pair
puttered the rainy fields in a rusty Jeep
and saw green waves of grass turn blue, the air
clear, bushes bloom, and vines run deep.
But they were only up to planting, bushes bare
and squat, when he died—buried on the steep
ancestral hill. She went on, day labor like a prayer
and every midnight climbing on the winding stair

to Yeats—Yeats all she read, night in, night out.
Is reading only Yeats the same as being mad? Abstract,
we feared she'd come to grief, wandering about
like Jane or Aengus, Gaelic fire in her head. We ransacked
our shelves—First Frost, then Wilbur as the antidote,
as beautiful, as deep, but *calm*. With patient Southern tact,
she'd smile, wait a week, and hand him back; devote
herself anew to Willie B, taking half of what he wrote

by heart, Brown Penny to Cold Heaven. Always finding more.
We thought she'd left us, abandoned for some acres and a book…
But I've re-read that year, now see what Yeats' spell was for:

Working the same hard ground and finding more was what it took.
Stitching intellect to intellect, and soul to soul, ancestral form
would rise and bloom from rows worked, and worked again. Look:
Children in the fields, berry baskets in their arms.
Yeats saved my friend that year, and my friend saved the farm.

Berkshire Summer

Recklessly, I grew attached to them.

That summer, everyone in town was eighty,
good looking, and smart. Oh, Sid was slow,
but he turned the women's heads
when he ambled into the gym,
and Nancy had the bones of a model
and a wicked laugh at her own infirm leg.
Paul thought like a scientist, precise,
complex, a little long-winded
describing his many intricate projects.
All of them had projects; the only thing
they couldn't do anymore was drive.

I drove, able to pretend
I was the generous youngster I'd been
so good at, offering an arm, opening a door,
pointing to a cracked step. Courtly,
with a bit of a bow
in the generosity of youth,
or even middle age, although
when I caught their eye
in the moment when gratitude and fear
were one, I had to count to ten
(ten? no, *thirteen*, years!)
not to hate them, hate the town
where old people held sway
as if it would always be their town.

We hung out that summer, me driving

to the terraced restaurants, raising a glass of wine
to their chic martinis, and together watching
the sun slip below the deep violet hills,
then driving home on the dark, familiar roads.

Coney Island Elegy

Curving in from the west, on the Belt, I pass
the Verrazano, children, dogs, fishermen and bikes

on the wide, seaside walk, under its Brooklyn arc, and beyond
I see the peninsula, like any small city

in the sun: towers, haze. The near projects are called
Gravesend, and this, Coney Island, is my country

churchyard. Inside the haze, the hidden streets
become particular: Cropsey, Neptune, Mermaid,

Surf. I cruise the empty avenues to see
down the decades to my first journey, to the war

on poverty I'd volunteered for, to the first proof
of myself in the street, of my own hands; to Marcia,

the friend I'd traveled with at twenty-one. I want to walk
then and now, knowing. I start with Stillwell,

where the trains stop. I park the car, and climb
the subway steps (elevated here) to broad cement

ramps and plazas, shuttered kiosks: a dream hotel
opening on a dozen halls and black exits.

(In dreams, this is where I am lost, but don't remember;
pursued, and don't know who.) But the dust of daylight

shafting through a high window, it's just the end of the line, terminus
of the D, the F, and the Sea Beach Express, my old way

home, the way to the Mermaid bus. As I walk it now,
Mermaid is as empty as at midnight then, but I conjure

the old carnival, the glimmering streetscape of streaks and pops
of primary color, people of color finger-popping

("This Old Heart of Mine," "Love Is Like—," "Beauty's Only—")
on the appointed corners. Fifteenth is the Italian-American

Social Club, a card table half out the door, a game
of endless odds, T-shirted men who have days to throw

dice. Seventeenth is the Coney Island Family Center ("People
working together will make things better"). A black

welfare mother struggles a stroller up the steps, laughing
at the soft, melodic tease of the Spanish teenager

on the stoop, stubbing out a Lucky. She's late
for the Mothers' Group, where she will stand and tell

how her first son Raymond had his head beaten, for nothing,
by the same ("Fat shark—") cop who got two other kids

here, on this almost-island, last week. It's '66; it is all
beginning: Cant is years away.   To stand, to give

common witness not to Jesus but to one's own daily life
is new, and makes light. "Any drugstore's ripped off for miles,

and he come with that stick, lookin'. For our kids." She lifts
her chin, and sits. Several people clasp, and unclasp, their hands,

hard, and one, brushing her skirt with a small fist, rises:
"We been pushed this far, out here with water on three sides.

Can't be pushed no more." The light of found voices unwalls
the crammed space. Marcia, in her green suit, sits, quiet,

on the stairs; palms a gold lighter; and watches, slowly.
Two weeks before, tutoring Vernell, she'd heard the latest,

bitter news (the cop, the kids), and said, "Let's get
the other mothers together." (Stamping out smoke after smoke,

one hourless night, she would test in new sentences a memory,
herself, and me: How, her elbows pinned, his breath a sulfur nail,

she had been taken, at twelve, her voice pinned in her throat,
jammed. How her deepest shame was her unvoicing, the rupture

at the core.) The mothers never said, "What the fuck
do you know, lady from Hood River, Oregon?" She was that

straight. So tonight they testify, and make some noise
that will bring the Mayor to this sea-locked strip,

with first promises. The echo of the Cyclone cuts in, and I turn
away from the illuminated room, off Mermaid, towards the shore.

Back of Surf, here, HUD's latest project has crushed

the old wood bungalows under thirty stories. Even then, the grey hut

had been a trick on time. The public appetite
for freaks had turned, the Side Show folded, fifteen years

before I sat, in a suede jacket and woolen hat, helping Louis
sift through shopping bags and coupons for his clinic card.

The room is full of magazines, the smell of kerosene and winter.
I am the outreach for lost cases, assigned: I listen. Once,

Louis, Donkey Boy, could headline, and his talk now
shuttles from those crowds—respect, to the surge of thoughts

that rouse him to the Boardwalk at 2 AM, to pace
and later, sleep there, with just the surf noise in his head.

He watches his hands stammer the last, unpronounceable sentence, then
grazes my eyes, embarrassment and pride in the monstrous smile.

We go to the clinic where his teeth are jimmied straight,
and now I stand in a thirty-story shadow, my hands dumb fists.

The new towers carom the wind, almost a low scream—
Home. I half run back to the Avenue, the flow of blood,

rhyme of feet on pavement restores the place to me. John's Bar
has its sign, but the open door where the Wurlitzer swirled

neon rhythms day and night is nailed. West 31st.
My stop. My block. The sneakers on the telephone wire

are a summer riddle I recognize (but never solved).
Only windows of air give away the first two apartment

houses, still two stories of brick, but no life:
neutroned. At 2864, I have to look again

to know how empty is the empty lot; I have to step
across the street to count. One, two, left; the schule,

right. So. It is anonymous debris back of
chicken wire. Even our tree is untraceable: no stump,

No root. I look for the baby, but there is only
broken glass. The first day, a one-armed baby in the crook

of the tree drew us (close up, a doll) to the little house
pitched left, as if floating on a flood. (I will dream a flood

floats the house free, and from the sinking roof, I will reach
for the children, Jerry, Eugene, Fred, and Sweetie Pie,

even Eleanor, lifting them: but as my hands close
on Jerry's wrist, Eleanor is sucked away, and in the center

of the vortex there is fire, and as they drown,
they burn; and the house drifts away

from hands, and their sound becomes the water's.)
But the dream is months ahead, and now (then) "4 rm apt

to let" fits the bill. We'd turned down ten decent
3 rm apts, Marcia, you and I, stuck

with each other (Vista's rule: no girls alone), each resolved
to have a door, to have her own year, to hold

her own. Where the pine cross holds chicken wire now,
we'd unlatched the chainlink gate, turned from the poor pink doll

angled in the tree, to the baby moving in the mud,
and the short, black-haired woman in a half-buttoned

sleeveless blouse, one eye askew. "Here's his number—
he's the landlord. Say Virginia sent you. He'll arrange it."

We arrange the things we own (books: Let Us Now
Praise Famous Men, Hopkins, mine; the Complete Shakespeare,

Inside Daisy Clover, yours; records: the MJQ, mine;
early Sinatra, yours; each one, to us, a precise choice)

in our own place.   Hair combed, Virginia comes for tea,
the children—Eugene, Jerry, Eleanor, Sweetie Pie

and Baby Fred—almost shiny. They play with everything.
Virginia's lucid, funny. We grin like fools. Next morning—

I am scanning this dirt for a trickle, a spring—
there is no water. No gas. After the third time

this happens (faucet's choke, dead stove) you take down
the coffee mugs, I crack the icetray into the electric frying pan
without a word. Virginia is outside, pounding a pipe
with a spoon, crouched in a muddy pool, digging in the dirt

for something lost. "Virginia's crazy;" the landlord
wipes his forehead and stares at the sweat on his palm.

"She tears the pipes apart." But later,
she is forking the ground with daffodil seed

as we pass carrying pails to fill up at Wayne's house.
Virginia pats the earth softly, and rocks and hums.

Now—a shoe, glass, and a broken door in some weeds
mark that spot. Eleven times the door is broken in.

Three times we're there, asleep, staring at intruders
as confused as we. It was never clear

what anyone was looking for, but we sit up those nights
taut before the picture window, facing two girls

smoking, stiff holds on broom handles, our faces
pale reflections floating on the night. The cops

come and go, shaking their heads. At dawn, we see through
the window—the tree, Mr. Haring's fish truck, a bird—and sleep.

We had jumped at the "thwuck!" The pigeon slams
into the picture window. Jerry gets there first. Back

at the kitchen table, the pigeon in a shoebox, Jerry blows
smokerings at the floor, ruffles his thick hair, and asks

"What happens to a pigeon when it dies?" I try, "I guess

if it's a good pigeon, it goes to heaven, and if it's bad

it goes to hell." Marcia gives me a look, and Jerry fixes me
with olive-black eyes as he snags a smokering

on one small, yellow finger: "How could a pigeon be bad?"
Together, we bury the pigeon, wrapped in a warm glove.

I notice the absence of pigeons, strays, scavengers,
boppers, and children. There were always the children.

Eugene (14) and Jerry (12) have IQs one SD either side
of 150, but they share one school shirt, required admission

to PS 81. Jerry gladly yields the shirt for his hooded
grey jacket, for the record he's working on: a hundred seventeen

consecutive absences. When his hair is cut, he comes up, hunched
under the grey hood. As you grab, he dives beneath the couch,

a sputter of giggles: "I've lost my strength!"
That night, you and I toast the year with two-dollar wine.

No water. No gas. Virginia is looking for the baby
she lost, the baby the pipes took; she is wrenching the pipes

with her hands. I call the landlord, you snap the ice, and Virginia
wanders up to show Eugene's report, a dazzle of A's held in bloody hands

Staking out the year, we held our own in Gravesend's
shadow, on the slim peninsula; but in the end, the fire-flood

came almost true. Pushing for the dozenth time
the unhinged door, expecting rifled clothes, the usual

dull ripoff, even a startled vagrant, we find everything we own
soaked in a viscous soup: syrup, then coffee grounds

and brown sugar, the chosen books buckled
and charred, the records a sick sand sculpture.

No torch, just the contents of cabinets, staples
spewed on hundreds of surfaces: The force

of ordinary substances uncontained. The children.
So they did violence to us, as we had done

violence to the scheme of things, like time-travelers,
the children knew, tampering with what was to be.

What was to be: The blocks ("Watch Coney Grow") deserted;
shelled. A gust up Surf from the shore scuds a beercan

by, and its long shadow takes our traces out of focus.
But in the last light, I see this: Jerry to school, twice

(a patter of jokes on the way, jabbing at the air, toughing it
out, then at the door a desperate look and in my hug,

for a flash, a boy). The Mothers. And you and me, raising toasts
and boiling ice, devising our own steady rituals,

taking hold, finding voice, meeting
the willed fear, and each other, squarely.

* * * *

It was not to be here, but on a good block, on the East Side:
the junkie and the knife, the stepping from the dark, flash of act
that in these disordered streets and years might have made
some sense; not here, but with your life intact

and won (*but far*) from practiced danger and the sweet rage
of our Coney Island days, you, companion on the first
passage, cease to be. So, as I came once for proof, and to gauge
the radius of my reach, I come for proof reversed,

and reach without measure; belief in disbelief—myth. No.
Our proving here was true—like the pigeon, the pipes, a grey
hood, hands, Louis fifteen years from the Side Show,
rooms lit by voices, ice—and will not betray

itself to wish, to my designs. A siren tells how randomly
mere arteries and skin surrender; and what is dark is clear:
how you leave the world to darkness, and to me
awhile, Marcia. We were here.

Hilde Weisert's poems have appeared in such publications as *The Cincinnati Review, Cortland Review, Prairie Schooner, Southern Poetry Review, The Sun, the NY Times, Ms, CALYX, Lips*, and the *Wilfred Owen Journal*. Honors and awards include a New Jersey State Arts Council Fellowship, a fellowship from the Virginia Center for the Creative Arts, the 2008 Lois Cranston Poetry Prize for "Finding Wilfred Owen Again, second prize in the 2014 Berkshire Festival of Women Writers for "The Pity of It," and honorable mentions in the 2013 Allen Ginsberg Poetry Awards, the 2015 Robert Frost Foundation Poetry Contest, and the 2015 New Millennium Writings Contest.

She worked for many years with the Geraldine Dodge Foundation as a Dodge Poet in the Schools, read at several Dodge Festivals, and edited *Teaching for Delight: a Compilation of ways of doing poetry in schools* published by the Dodge Poetry Project. She is a co-founder of the Society for Veterinary Medicine and Literature, which co-sponsored the first international conference on Veterinary Medicine and Literature in 2010 in Guelph, Ontario with Ontario Veterinary College.

Weisert is co-editor of the 2012 anthology *Animal Companions, Animal Doctors, Animal People: Poems, essays, and stories on our essential connections* published by Ontario Veterinary College, University of Guelph.

Hilde Weisert was raised in Chicago, Illinois, Washington, DC, and France, and now lives part-time in Chapel Hill, NC and Sandisfield, MA.

CPSIA information can be obtained
at www.ICGtesting.com
Printed in the USA
FFOW01n1733181215
19529FF